James Adair

Discussions of the Law of Libels as at Present Received

in Which its Authenticity is Examined...

James Adair

Discussions of the Law of Libels as at Present Received
in Which its Authenticity is Examined...

ISBN/EAN: 9783337280826

Printed in Europe, USA, Canada, Australia, Japan

Cover: Foto ©Suzi / pixelio.de

More available books at **www.hansebooks.com**

DISCUSSIONS

OF THE

LAW OF LIBELS

AS AT PRESENT RECEIVED,

IN WHICH ITS

AUTHENTICITY

IS

EXAMINED;

WITH

INCIDENTAL OBSERVATIONS

ON THE

LEGAL EFFECT

OF

PRECEDENT AND AUTHORITY.

LONDON:
PRINTED FOR T. CADELL, IN THE STRAND.
M. DCC. LXXXV.

Passages from the Private Correspondence of the Editor.

" WITH respect to the publication in question, you admit, I think, that the substance of our conferences is, upon the whole, faithfully preserved.—This is all I ask.—You must then allow it at least, the merit of containing the law itself, with your Readings upon it: it may also have that of proving its successful resistance to the cavils of the captious objector.

" You still suspect that more accurate researches in the history of our law would evince, that this doctrine has a higher original and more authentic sanction than I attribute to it; and that the argument on your side has not all the advantage to which it is fairly entitled. You have however, had recourse to the topics upon which it is generally supported; and you will observe, that my reasoning has for its object, not only to shew that it is not law, but that if it is law it ought no longer to remain so.

" I may admit libel to be a public offence, but I may at the same time doubt the authenticity of your doctrine in its extent: I may admit the authenticity of your doctrine in its extent, and still question its justice.

" Your conjectures have, however, suggested the necessity of a more particular investigation of the subject; and, I own, I cannot after all discover upon what ground of authority Lord Coke lays down his doctrine as the common law of England.

" From the laws of the West-Saxons which were probably afterwards incorpo-
rated

rated into the general code founded by Alfred, and restored by Edward the Confessor, it appears [a] indeed that penalties strongly tinctured with the barbarism of the age, were inflicted upon the *calumniator*. Lord Coke [b] has also cited laws of Alured, Edgar, and Canute which clearly prove this point. But it is to be observed that even in those times the offence consisted in the *falsehood* of the calumny. I must also remark, that had the law of slander, as at present received, derived itself from so remote an origin it is manifest that every species of slander would have been *penal*; and that *penal* slander might have been *justified*. But we know that by our law every species of slander is not penal; and that by the law, as delivered by Lord Coke, the *truth* of penal slander, or libel, is no justification of it.

" To this doctrine, which professes to be the common law of the country,

[a] Lambard Archaionomia.   [b] 2 Inst. 227.

no support is derived from the *mirror, Britton, Fleta,* or *Fitzherbert* no ornament [c] from *Glanville* or *Bracton.*

" From *Britton,* I find indeed among the articles of public offence, which were required to be presented before the justices of *Eyre,* the *devising* and reporting *false* rumours concerning the king, *ceux qui trouvent & content* mensonges *de nous* [d].

In Fleta mention is made " *de inventoribus malorum rumorum, unde pax possit exterminari* [e].

It appears also that in the time of Edward the First special commissions were sent to all the counties of England, " *de rege* purgando *de certis numoribus iniquis contra ipsum ortis* [f].

[c] Plowden 357.   [d] Britton 33.
[e] Fleta, l. 2. c. 1.   [f] 2 Inst. 227.

These

These provisions, it is evident, relate to offences against the government or against the public peace: offences of a very different class [g] from that to which the offence we are considering, belongs, and in all of them the slander must be false.

" The passage cited from *Bracton*, by *Lord Coke* in support of his doctrine, appears to be misapplied. From the context, and from the division under which it appears, it is evident that writer is not speaking of criminal offences, one might rather infer, that he considered libel as a mere civil injury [h].

" I have not, after all, been able to trace up the general doctrine, we are considering to a higher source than that from which the following discussions

[g] Page 46. [h] 9 Co. 6. Bract de Cor. 155.

suppose it to be derived, Lord Coke's report of the decision of the Star-Chamber in the famous case of libels.

" From the materials I have communicated to you the outline of my design will suggest itself.

" The present discussions confine themselves to the law of libels upon private persons. This doctrine however is extended not only to libels upon public persons but to criminal publications in general.

" In a future publication, which will treat more particularly of the judicial cognisance of the offence, the general reasoning I have employed will itself furnish its necessary qualifications. I shall then admit that there are possible cases in which the criminal intent of a publication is not disproved by the truth of the facts it contains, I shall also admit that there are like-

likewife poffible cafes in which public decency could not permit the truth of a publication to be proved in evidence. Thefe exceptions are, however, not inconfiftent with the fpirit of that reafoning, by which I have endeavoured to fhew, that a court of juftice cannot in general form a competent judgment of the intent of a publication, if it be precluded from the examination of its truth or falfhood.

"So much for the *matter* of this publication,—as to the reft, in the friendly feverity of your criticifm, you ought to remember that I profefs only to give a converfation upon paper.

"You remark, I hope, that I have endeavoured to obferve, a fort of *dramatic keeping* in the characters we refpectively fuftain.—I the legal fceptic—you the profeffional optimift—you grave, folemn, and decorous—I, inquifitive, impatient, and petulant. In the choice of the very types

types by which our parts are marked to the eye, I did not lose sight of this distinction. There is something in the *sombre* cast and self-involved character of the old black letter which must strike you as not ill contrasted with the light, flimsy, and unsubstantial texture of that of modern innovation.

" I cannot conclude without confessing that I feel very strongly the force of an observation in your letter.—When I consider with you the length of time this doctrine has prevailed—the sanction it has received from liberal and enlightened judges—and above all, that it has stood the trial of the revolution itself—I must, perhaps, own, that the errors of it are grown so inveterate as to be remediable not by a *judicial*, but by a *legislative* interposition alone."

CONTENTS.

Examination of the authenticity of this law.

THE famous cafe of libels in the ftar-chamber its immediate origin.

The authority of Lord Coke, and the precedents he has produced in fupport of it.

Authority and precedent in general prefumptive evidence of law.

The evidence of general principles.

The evidence produced in fupport of the general doctrine defective: and hence the neceffity of referring its authenticity to an examination by general principles.

The question stated, and mode of discussion proposed.

From p. 1. to p. 26.

The constitution of the offence of libel considered.

The considerations which render it a public injury.

The presumption of injury to the character of the individual.

The presumption of the individual's resentment—of that of his family, friends, and connections.

The presumption of violence in consequence of such resentment.

The

CONTENTS.

The prefumption of a difturbance of the public peace.

The neceffity of public redrefs to the injury induced by the above confiderations.

Spiritual—civil—criminal—defamation diftinguifhed.

The criminal form of the offence—the writing or printing—the publication.

The poffibility of the injury to the public morals, manners, and decency; and of the direct injury to the public peace, by the mean of a defamatory libel on the individual.

From p. 27. to p. 28.

The truth or falsehood of the libel.

The position that "the libel not the less a libel for its being true," considered with respect

To justice and policy;

To the general sense of the unwritten law as collected from the letter, spirit, and judicial construction of the statutes *de scandalis magnatum.*

To the sense of the court itself in which the offence is cognizable as collected from its practice.

From p. 58, to p. 97.

The

CONTENTS.

———————

The case de Libellis Famosis, 5. Co. 25. is subjoined.

ERRATA.

P. 6. l. 18. read you *who* debase.
   8.   4. leave out the comma after *chapter*.
   9.   4. read *its*, instead of *it is*.
  15. 11. read *lex*, instead of *len*.
  20.   2. read *waive*, instead of *wave*.
  64. 17. read *a* strange.

DISCUSSIONS, &c.

L. I Plead to the jurisdiction;—I deny it's competency.—The issue of this great question must be tried by the law of the land alone. When I call for that law, you read me the *decision of a court, the principle of whose constitution, the rules of whose proceeding, the spirit of whose judgments were in perpetual conflict with it.

* The case de *Libellis Famosis*, 5 Co. 125.

L. I do not produce this Star-Chamber determination, for it's intrinsic merit only, but for the sanction the doctrine contained in it, receives from the concurrent opinion of that great oracle of our law, the Lord Coke.

L. The responses of that oracle, like those of other oracles, were sometimes prompted by the personal policy of the prince, and the ambition of the minister. His extensive professional learning gives great weight to his opinion on all occasions; but there are some in which his interest must be placed in the opposing scale.—When I consider the ascendancy of the prerogative at the time in which he lived, I do not feel myself disposed implicitly to subscribe to his sentiments, on a question which in certain respects contrasted the power of government with the liberty of the subject. The true value of of his opinion in every cafe muft be eftimated by the teft of "reafon and the "franchife of the land."

L. This is his own fentiment;—and you pay an involuntary tribute to his memory, when to refift his authority, you are obliged to have recourfe to the arms himfelf has furnifhed.

L. It is true;. I cite Lord Coke againft himfelf;—I appeal from Lord Coke the courtly judge, to Lord Coke the patriot Englifh lawyer. I repeat it, I mean to eftimate, not to depreciate his authority. And if I were to delineate his moral character, I would wifh to view it, not in the meridian funfhine, but in the mild evening of his day. I fhould defire to forget his invectives againft Effex and Raleigh; and to remember only that he afterwards oppofed the meafures of defpotifm,

potifm, that he drew and propofed the petition of right. When I fee him fuffering under the fangs of the prerogative, " that overgrown monfter," as he then calls it, I wifh not to mix with the emotions I feel a malignant pleafure from the reflecting, that he had himfelf affifted to rear it

All I intend at prefent is to enquire whether there was any juft caufe for the king's command delivered to him at the council, in the hour of his difgrace, by Winwood. The fecretary enjoins him " to review, in his retirement, his books " of reports," wherein he tells him, " his " majefty was informed, there were many " extravagant and exorbitant opinions fet " down for pofitive and good law."

L. This calumny was probably inftilled in the ear of James by Lord Coke's enemy,

enemy; the attorney general, afterwards Lord Bacon.

L. The calumny I admit to have been in general false; I wish only to examine whether it had not some foundation in the present instance: though this perhaps is not one of the cases to which the king's command was meant to be applied.

L. You will however observe, that his doctrine on this subject does not rest merely upon its own authority: in support of it he has produced precedents of so early a date, as the reign of Edward the Third.

L. Among the precedents of that reign, there is one which gives us the outline of the proceeding of the Court of King's Bench, against sorcerers. I take it from Hawkins* and will read it to you.—

* Pleas of the Crown, B. 1. C. 3.

L. You

L. You need not; I recollect it perfectly well: but the law is now obsolete.

L. We have, it is true, no more sorcerers; the law has ceased with the object of it: should this art, however, be restored, you would not, I think, propose the precedent as a correct model of the judicial cognizance of it.

L. This is an unbecoming sneer;— impeach the authority of precedents, and you render vain and illusory the boast " of being governed by known laws."

L. I wish to maintain this glorious privilege, by fixing it on the firm and consistent basis of reason. The excellency of laws does not merely consist in their being known, but in their justice and equality— It is you debase the authority of precedents, by the blind and implicit confidence

dence you exact to it; not I who desire my faith to be enlightened.

L. I do not attribute infallibility to the judgments of our courts; on the contrary, I know that former precedents have been frequently declared in subsequent decisions of the same points, " not " to be law." And I know too, that the general practice of every court, and the right of appeal from one to the other, suppose the possibility of error. But observe the course I have taken;—I indeed admit to you, that the law, as received at present, on this subject, derives itself immediately from the report of a decision of the Star Chamber, the famous case of libels; but I assert, that this decision was declaratory of the common law, as it then existed, and in proof of this assertion I offer the opinion of the reporter, and the precedents to which he refers.

What

What is the nature of the evidence you require?

L. I certainly do not expect that you should produce a chapter, from the compilations of Edward the Confessor, a fragment of the dome-book of Alfred, or a stanza from the songs of the Druids. If you were to produce the law itself, you would, in the language of the profession be non-suit; since you have undertaken to establish it by immemorial usage alone. And in support of that usage I cannot I know, require any other sort of proof than that which you bring. I admit, that in questions of this nature, precedents and authorities are strong presumptive evidence of law: as such, they indeed become conclusive when unencountered by superior evidence; but as such too, by the force of superior evidence their effect may be defeated.

L. And what do you confider as the evidence fuperior to that of precedent?

L. That which is deduced from the law itfelf; the evidence of it is reafon.

L. And whence do you collect the reafon of the law?

L. From its eftablifhed principles.

L. And thefe eftablifhed principles, what gives them their ftamp and currency?

L. The general obfervance of them in judicial decifions.

L. That is, in precedents; you are reduced to the necessity of confessing the authority of precedents, in the very instant in which you controvert it; to precedents you oppose precedents.

L. I oppose evidence to evidence; I oppose the evidence of precedents in general (for principles are abstractions from precedents in general) to the evidence of one or more. And in this the law is consistent; its respect for the authority of precedents is the very reason, why the greater number have more weight with it than the less.

L. I do not disapprove of your idea; on the contrary I wish to fix it, as I hope to avail myself of it hereafter. It is not then, the suggestions of general reasoning, unexercised in, and unapplied to,

the

the science of the law that you would oppose to the authority of precedents?

L. Certainly not; but the reason that arises from a systematic view of it.

L. And the precedents of which the reason has ceased, or for which the reason does not appear, or which general reasoning may perhaps disapprove, but against which no reason can be drawn from the law itself, ought still, you conceive, to be supported.

L. Exactly so; the law, if I may be allowed the expression, observes no neutrality on such occasions. If it is not against a precedent it is with it, and it frequently happens that it protects a decision which perhaps from its own weakness could not defend itself; and that, upon this principle of sound policy, that the error of one precedent is rather to be endured, than the uncertainty of all.

L. It would then follow, that in a question upon the unwritten law, a court would be as much bound by the rule which precedent had established, even though it should not approve of it, as it would be in a question of written law, by a positive act of parliament, the impolicy of which might be manifest.

L. You are fixing me indeed!

L. The consequence is inevitable from your own premises.

L. With the qualifications I have annexed, I believe I may admit it. The court, in the consideration of an adjudged case, cannot, I think, regard the in-

inconvenience or harshness of its operation, in the particular instance before it: it can only examine, whether it be or not legally *inconvenient*; consistent or inconsistent with the principles of that system, of which it professes to form a part. The upright judge, impressed with the religion of his high office, pronounces that judgment, not which his private reason, but which his duty suggests,—*perquam durum est sed ita len est*. I have, I hope, sufficiently explained myself.

L. You have indeed conceded to me more than I expected, and have so completely assisted me in the fortifying my position, that I cannot discover, in what quarter a breach is practicable.

L. The metaphor is not germain to the subject. For the purpose of illustrating my idea, and of placing your arguments in in their true point of view, allow me an allusion with which the nature of our enquiry has more affinity.

You have set out your custom upon the record; you have opened your case, and the evidence by which you intend to support it. To your Star-Chamber determination I object, that it is not a court of competent jurisdiction; the judgment is not conclusive. As your first witness you call I think Lord Coke.

L. Whom you consistently with your objection to his interest mean I suppose to examine upon a *voir dire*.

L. I always wish to hear Lord Coke; my objection does not go to his *competency* but merely to his *credit*. For your next evidence you offer two precedents.

L. You will not I hope aver *against the record.*

L. Certainly not; one of them does not conclude for you; and the other concludes against you.

L. I propose in the next place, to produce a cloud of as respectable witnesses as ever appeared in a court of justice.

L. Not I hope to the general character and credit of your first witness; have I impeached it?

L. I mean a series of authorities and decisions *since* the time of Lord Coke to the present moment.

L. However highly I may deem of the great names which have sanctioned those authorities and those decisions, I cannot allow you to avail yourself of their testimony; it does not meet the point of the question: for you have undertaken to prove that your law existed *before* the time of Lord Coke. If you cannot shew this, the doctrine contained in the resolutions of your Star-Chamber case is not law; unless you mean to contend that the pronouncing it made it so. But I am sure, whatever might be the arrogations of that court, you are too good an Englishman, to allow it to have had a legislative authority.

L. I have not sufficiently prepared myself with evidence from that period, to which

which, I admit, the question is in its present shape confined.

L. Perhaps the search may be unnecessary;—let us however examine the precedents * you have produced. Upon the first I observe, that it is incomplete; the judgment does not appear. As it is at present, it only proves that it was the opinion of the prosecutor, that the offence was indictable; but it does not shew that this was the opinion of the court, on the contrary, one might infer, if no judgment was pronounced, that it was the opinion of the court, that it was not an indictable offence.

But, admitting that judgment actually passed, still I observe that this is not evidence of that full and decisive effect, which the importance of the question requires. I should have expected the production of

* 3 Inst. 174.

a record in which the point had been determined, after argument and solemn consideration, upon demurrer or arrest of judgment. This case may have proceeded, according to your own Lord Coke's expression, "without challenge of the party or debate of the justices."

I apply this last observation to your other precedent; but allowing it its full force it makes against you. The judgment indeed appears, but unfortunately contradicts your first witness, and concludes against the allegation of your custom, "that * the truth or falsehood of the libel is immaterial to the nature of the offence. For the falsehood of the libel is stated as the ground of the judgment; *quæ litera continet in se nullam veritatem* §." And it does not prove that which your custom also alleges, that a penalty was

* 5 Co. 125.   § 3 Inst. 174.

by

by the common law annexed to the offence*. For though the libel in this case is declared to have a tendency "*in scandalum justiciariorum et curiæ*, to scandalise the public justice of the country," the court, as I understand the judgment, only directs that security shall be taken for the good behaviour of the defendant: from whence one might infer that *prevention* and not *punishment* was the common law remedy for the offence.

L. But what evidence do you oppose to that I have offered?

L. I doubt whether you have made such a case as entitles you to call upon me for an answer. Your evidence is not only defective, but contradictory; and

---

* 5 Co. 125.

destroys the very custom it affects to support. But I wave my objection to that which you have already produced, or may hereafter produce. The error I assign is upon the face of the record. The custom you have set out is unreasonable; it destroys itself.

The law you advance professes to derive itself from a period of antiquity, at which, from the general ignorance of the arts, not only of printing, but of writing, the offence of libel, which, as you define it, consists in written or printed defamation, was scarcely possible. Certain it is, that it could not be of sufficient frequency to engage the attention of the legislature. I do not so much insist upon this observation,

vation, becaufe, at whatever period it might obtain, this law, (I repeat the expreffion) is " againft reafon and the fran- " chife of the land."

L. Allow me to interrupt you. Do you mean to contend that no practice can be an offence by the unwritten law, but that which muft have had a neceffary and frequent occurrence, in that period of remote antiquity, from which fome of our common-law cuftoms are fuppofed to derive their origin? I think you might as well infift, that the deftroying a man by fire-arms, was not capital by the law of the twelfth century, becaufe gunpowder was not invented till the thirteenth; that poifoning with laurel-water was not murder, becaufe the knowledge of it's deleterious effects is a recent difcovery; or that a nuifance cannot be committed by a preparation which infects the common

common air, becaufe the relative properties of its ingredients, have been newly found out by the chymift.

L. Every malicious deftruction of the life of the individual is murder; every injury to the public health is nuifance. But if you were afferting the exiftence of a law in the twelfth century, which made the ufe of fire-arms in every cafe penal; or which before the noxious qualities of the diftillation you inftance were known, prohibited the adminiftering it in medicine; or which, to meet your third cafe, before the unwholefome effects of your chymical preparation had been difcovered, declared the experiment a nuifance; I fhould object, as I do now, that the law defeated itfelf, that its exiftence was not fuppofeable.

L. You

L. You say that every injury to the public health is a nuisance;—whence, I ask you, do you derive the sanction of that law, but from judicial decisions?

L. It is impossible not to admit, that a great part of our law owes its immediate original to judicial declarations; but it is also to be traced up, as to its source, to the first principles of the law and government of this country, from which such decisions are the unforced derivations.

L. This is precisely the point to which I wished to lead you:—And why may not the law in question have been so derived?

L. You have I think, taken another course—you profess to derive it, not from the general principles of the law, but from a positive constitution, by which
libel

libel was made an offence, and a specific penalty annexed to it. But whichever of these courses you take, my objection meets you; as I am to maintain that your law is unreasonable, in the strict sense we have before annexed to the term. For observe.—As you do not produce the law itself, you must necessarily proceed in one of these ways;—either you offer your authorities and precedents, to induce a presumption that the law once existed;—or you produce them as deductions, from the general principles of our system. In the first instance, I oppose evidence to evidence,—to your authorities and precedents general principles; and I say, that the presumption against its having existed is stronger than the presumption for it.

In the second instance, I answer, that the law you suppose, is, not only not derivable from, but absolutely inconsistent with the principles of our law.

In

In either view, therefore, the enquiry refolves itfelf into this queftion:—whether the law as received upon this fubject, be deducible from the general principles of our legal fyftem?—you engage fo to deduce it;—I am to maintain that it is inconfiftent with them. And as in a queftion of private right, our reafonings would be drawn from the civil department of it; fo in a queftion of public wrong, they muft be drawn from its criminal department. If the precedents and authorities you can produce have the fanction of thefe principles, I admit the juft effect of them; but againft thefe principles they cannot, I think, prevail.

L. I consent that the discussion proceed upon this state of the question:—you have however, I suspect, formed a hasty and rash conclusion.

Tecum habita et noris quam sit libi curta supellex.

L. I do not pronounce;—I wish only to examine. In return for your advice, let me cite you an observation, which, to each of us, may suggest an useful lesson. The chancellor d'Aguesseau in the conclusion of his instructions to his son, on the study of history, has this passage, " ceuxcy veulent juger de ce qui s'est fait, " par ce qui doit se faire; et ceux la " veulent toujours décider de ce qui doit " se faire par ce qui se fait. Les uns " font, si je l'ose dire, la dupe des raison- " nemens, et les autres le font des faits " qu'ils prennent pour la raison meme."

L. The

L. THE character of this offence, as you describe it*, has rather an anomalous appearance ;—your definition does not necessarily require it to have been attended with actual injury to the public: the injurious public consequences of it are not positive, but merely presumptive. It is, in this respect, I think, distinguishable from offences in general which consist rather in the injury itself, than in the bare tendency to it. Other offences require realities to their composi-

* Hawkins's Pleas of the Crown, b 1 c. 73. § 1. 3.

tion, this is wholly compofed of prefumptions and probabilities.

Defamation is, I admit, in itfelf an immorality, and evidently proceeds from a heart regardlefs of focial duty. In its confequences too it may be a civil injury. But all immoralities, all civil injuries are not crimes: what then is the confideration which in the view of government, renders it a public offence?

L. It has been in moft governments fo treated. The offence of libel by the law of the twelve tables——

L. Non a duodecium tabulis, neque a prætoris edicto, fed penitus ex intima philofophiâ hauriendam juris difciplinam puto. We are confidering the nature of the offence itfelf, not the arbitrary conftitution of it in different governments, or the penalties they may have annexed to it; penalties which have been too frequently

mea-

measured, not by the exigency of the offence itself, but by the passions and sinister policy of those who governed. In the middle age of Rome, it was subjected to corporal punishment; but the extremes of political tyranny met; the Decemvirs and the Emperor Valentinian punished it with death.

L. In modern Europe the French Law——

L. Is the law of that government: we are considering the genius of our own.

L. And in our own (for I think I too hastily gave up my former argument) I am persuaded that researches in its history would shew——

L. That this offence has been punished with the disgracing and mangling the
human

human form,—with such horrors and infamies, that all recollection of the injury was lost in the barbarity of the punishment.—" Men," says Lord Clarendon, " begun no more to consider the former " manners of the offenders, but the " men."

I wish to confine you to that course of enquiry, to which you have yourself consented, to the derivation of your doctrine, not from the laws of other countries, but from the principles of our own; not from the practice of other governments, nor even from that of our own, in some periods of it, but from the enlightened spirit of it. And I pause upon the very outset of the discussion, for a reason in which I may, perhaps be singular. I doubt whether the mere defamation of the subject can, upon the principles of our government, ever be a public offence. I admit, that the injurious practice ought to be restrained, but I hesitate upon the means. I doubt whether it ought not in all cases, to be punished by a civil action, if I may use the expression, rather than by a criminal proceeding; whether the penalty ought not to be rather compensation to the private party, than vindictive satisfaction to the public party. At least the former appears to me more consonant to the genius of our law and our government than the latter.

It is, I think, the spirit of arbitrary governments to prefer public punishment to civil compensation. Jealous of his power, the Despot seeks not so much reparation of the injury to the individual, as an atonement for the affront to his authority. Such a government, is in truth, more anxious for the maintenance of its enormous arrogations, than for the protection of the just rights of the subject.

L. You

L. You do not advert to the peculiar nature of the offence.

L. It is indeed the peculiar nature of the offence, that accounts for its having been fingled out as the object of the difproportionate penalties which have been inflicted upon it. The motive of them has been not fo much to protect the character of the individual, as that of the government itfelf from cenfure. From a dread that the shaft of juft reproach might in fome inftance glance too high, the ufe of it in every inftance has been feverely prohibited.

L. You forget its tendency to difturb the public tranquillity.

L. The public tranquillity, as it is the only fecurity of an arbitrary government,

is

is the object to which it sacrifices every other. The apprehension of a disturbance of the public peace, from the resentment of the individual is, I think, rather imputable to the suspicious vigilance and timidity of a bad government, than to the firmness of a good one.

I think I perfectly well understand the spirit of Lord Coke's eulogium, on the court of Star-Chamber, " This court, " the right institution and antient orders " thereof being observed, doth keep all " England in quiet *"; I think I comprehend the principle, upon which this court affected the criminal cognizance of a civil injury;—made the sensibility of the injured party, the measure, not of its reparation, but of its vindictive satisfaction;—discovered in his possible resentments, a possible disturbance of the public

* 4 Inst. c. 5.

peace, and administered to it not prevention but punishment.

When I read the famous case of libels, I own I am not surprized that the learned reporter gives us declamation in the place of sober reason. But the premises of the doctrine of that case once granted, I must admit, I know, the consequences that follow from them. When your authority asserts * "that it is not material, whe-" ther the libel be true, or whether the "party against whom the libel is made be "of good or ill fame," I may doubt the legality of the position: but when I read that a libel upon persons entrusted with the administration of government is a still greater offence, I understand the use of the argument *a fortiori*, and feel all the force of the inevitable conclusion. In the darkest pages of our history I collect the

* 5. Co. 125.

purposes

purposes of this institution from the purposes to which it has actually been employed.

L. The order of a good government I still think requires the punishment of this offence; for, if there were no public redress for the injury*, the injured party could not be restrained from acts of violence. The law allows, in many cases, no other remedy for libel.

L. The order of good government requires such a system of justice, that no public wrong shall be without its punish-

* 1 Hawk. P. C. 73.

ment, no private wrong without its compenfation. This fyftem once complete, the private party who takes the punifhment of wrong into his own hands, is an ufurper of the public authority: and this the law cannot pre-fuppofe.

L. But upon what other principle does government take cognizance of any injury whatever, but upon that of preventing the diforder that would enfue, from the individual's righting himfelf?

L. This is certainly the motive upon which government not only punifhes the public injury, but compenfates the private one. But, before this principle can have its application, the act itfelf muft from its nature be an injury public or private. Inftead of the criminal ingredient of this offence, you fubftitute the general motive of government to the punifhing of all offences

fences whatever. I will illuftrate my meaning.

If I were to afk, why murder is an offence; in the fpirit of your reafoning you might anfwer, becaufe, if it were not punifhed, the relation or friend of the deceafed, might be inflamed to avenge his death; violence and diforder might enfue.—To this I fhould then obferve, this is not the circumftance which conftitutes the crime, this is the motive of government to the punifhing an act which is in itfelf an injury to fociety, the extinction of a life in which it is directly interefted.

Again, if I were to afk, why government enforces a compenfation for an injury to the private rights of the individual; you might alfo anfwer, to prevent the party claiming it, from compelling a reparation by force. Here likewife I fhould remark,

remark, this is merely the motive of government, for exacting a satisfaction for the violation of a right which it recognises. But I should not complicate a public offence in this manner: I should not say this act is in its nature an injury to the individual; but it is an injury for which the law gives no satisfaction; and the law giving no satisfaction for it, it is possible the injured party may compel it by force; and because the injured party may compel it by force, this act has a tendency to a breach of the peace; and because it has a tendency to a breach of the peace, this act is a public offence.

L. Do you then mean to contend, that this species of defamation ought in all cases to be remediable by civil redress?

L. It is not necessary to my argument that I should contend for so much.—You are to shew it a public offence.

Upon

Upon the first view of this offence, as you define it, one might be inclined to rank it in the class of actionable injuries. " The exposing the individual to the contempt or hatred of mankind," one might think cannot but be injurious to his comfort and happiness; a damage which seems as estimable by compensation as many others for which it is enforced. Considered in another respect, the injury becomes still more palpable to such an estimation; the good name of the individual is a valuable possession; it is in every rank of life, if not property itself, the means of acquiring it. It is not I, however, it is you who are reduced to the necessity of confessing it in all cases, in which it is criminally cognisable a civil injury. It is you, who for the purpose of raising it to an importance sufficient to engage the attention of government, describe it as the highest of injuries to the individual, and of all others the most sensibly senfibly felt by him. And you cannot do this, without imputing the not having provided civil redrefs for it, as a defect in our fyftem; but you do worfe—you reprefent the law as availing itfelf of this very defect, for the purpofe of making the act a public offence. Produce me another inftance of an offence fo conftituted by our law.

L. I may admit the cafe to be anomalous; but the injury is fo too. It is fuch as the law cannot but recognife, and at the fame time fuch as cannot always be the fubject of civil fatisfaction.

L. But

L. But in cafes where defamation is not remediable by action, is it not cognifable by fuit in the fpiritual court?

L. If it import a charge of an offence *there* punifhable.

L. The fyftem then feems to me to be complete. Where-ever the law can take notice of the defamation, it appears to have provided adequate remedy: for the moral injury the fpiritual proceeding; for the civil injury the proceeding by civil action. What then remains for the criminal proceeding?

L. The writing, or printing the defamation.

L. But the writing or printing does not take it out of civil cognifance. Libel,

bel, if it contain actionable slander, is still actionable.

L. But it takes it out of the cognisance of the spiritual court.

L. Upon what principle ?—does the defamation become from this circumstance less immoral or less irreligious ?

L. Upon this principle, that it is indictable at common law.

L. This is indeed a reason. Your argument " is come full circle."

I observe however, that your reason from the want of redress is not co-extensive with your law; it does not prevail in those cases of libel for which there is a remedy by action.

L. Still

L. Still you muſt admit, that it ought to prevail where the law gives no ſuch remedy.

L. The conſequence is by no means neceſſary. If the injury be ſubſtantial enough, for the preſumption of damage to the individual to attach upon it, it is ſubſtantial enough for compenſation ; if it be not—*omnia ſcire, non omnia reſequi.*

A moment's recollection will, I think, ſuggeſt to you inſtances of "heart-ſtruck "injuries" to the individual of which our law takes no cogniſance, and of which, not taking cogniſance of them, it will not intend the reſentment by violence. But, in the way in which you proceed, there is no breach of honor or duty from man to man, which may not, from the provoking quality of it, and the probability of its being reſented, be rendered a public offence. Nay, more—

upon your principle all those affronts, which in the sense of modern honor, are considered as signals for an appeal to the " trial by battle," become criminally cognisable. The law, I know, cannot regard the provocation in such cases; but I leave it to you to reconcile the inconsistency of presuming the resentment, where it is at most only probable, and of not recognising it, where the custom of the age has rendered it almost certain.

Observe, however, another extravagent consequence from your doctrine. You maintain, that the offence in every case, consists in the tendency to excite the resentment of it. The judicial application of this principle, I remark, is impossible. For a court cannot in the very instant in which it is administering public redress for the injury, proceed upon a supposition of the possibility of the injured party's resenting it himself. The moment

moment the injury is conſtituted a public offence, there is an end of its tendency to a breach of the peace, by the violence of the injured party. You make that a criminal ingredient of the offence which cannot, in any given caſe, be taken into the judicial conſideration of it.

L. Are you then contending, that in our law no act is conſtituted an offence, by its tendency to a diſturbance of the public peace?

L. Moſt unqueſtionably I am not ſo contending;—but I think I ſhall ſhew a manifeſt diſtinction between this offence and thoſe of that claſs.

At

At present you appear to me however, to confound two ideas, which are in our law perfectly distinct. Every subject of the government is entitled to its protection: he is said to be in the king's peace; because the king is the executive magistrate of the government. Hence every violence to his person is charged as an offence, " against the peace of our so-" vereign lord the king." But an offence against the public peace, I consider to be of a very different nature. It does not merely consist in an injury to the peace or protection of one individual, but to the peace or security of all individuals. Every act which has the effect of exciting general terror and alarm, is certainly an offence against the public peace, and as such properly punishable; but the act which has a tendency to a mere breach of the peace, in the person of the individual the law does not consider as the subject

ject of *punishment*, but of *prevention*. For even where intended violence to any one is manifested by direct and positive menaces, the law does not punish such intention, but merely takes security that it shall not be committed, not from the party, against whom, but from whom it is apprehended. In this case the party is punished who is presumed to have excited a resentment, of which himself is to be the object.

L. You forget that the scandal may excite not only the resentment of the party injured, but of his family, his friends, and connexions.

L. And produce a sort of *chaude-melée* among them all. The law proceeds in no case

case upon so *foreign* a presumption; if it did, it would, I think, administer the remedy I have mentioned. Again I challenge you to produce another instance of an offence so constituted.

L. Your expression suggests one somewhat analogous to the present; *challenges to fight* are criminal by our law.

L. The cases may be somewhat analogous, but at the same time, you must allow, that they are somewhat dissimilar.

The one is a *direct* and *positive* solicitation to join in an act, the avowed purpose of which is the destruction of the individual, with which solicitation, the custom and manners of the age render a compliance more than probable.

The other is a *constructive* invitation to an individual, his family, and friends

to

to form a party, in which the inviter is not to beat, but is to be beaten,—*ubi vos pulsatis ego vapulo tantum*—which invitation, as these *ex parte* engagements are not fashionable, is generally declined.

L. Your pleasantry is rather misplaced; but am I to understand you to insist that the defamation of the individual, can in no case have a tendency to disturb the public peace? for you have admitted, I think, that this circumstance would render it a public offence.

L. All I mean to maintain is, that defamation of itself cannot be a public offence; it may be so I allow in its consequences. And though I consider the general doctrine you advance as unsupportable, yet I think you might have defended it upon more plausible reasoning. If you had assigned to the scandal, the tendency

tendency of exciting resentment and violence, not against the party defaming, but against the object of the defamation, there would have been some colour for the argument. You might then have proceeded in this way:—Defamation civilly cognisable, is that which has the effect of debasing the individual, who is the object of it in the estimation of society;—but if, added to this effect, it has that of exciting mankind to acts of hostility against him, it becomes criminal. I should then have admitted, as I now admit, that the publication of a scandal which had for its evident purpose, to inflame the passions or prejudices of the public against the object of it, would be a public offence: but I should then deny, as I now deny, that such an effect was in general, assignable to the defamation of the individual.

The

The actual conjuncture of the times, the nature of the defamation, the situation and character of the object of it, may render a scandalous publication as effectual a mean of disturbing the public peace as any other. The case however must be examined upon its own particular circumstances, which, as they would be of the criminal essence of the charge, must be averred and proved. But it is evident that the offence would consist in something very different from the presumption of the party's himself resenting the injury.

L. I need not of course ask you, whether you admit that a libel upon the character of the deceased can be a public offence.

L. Certainly not of itself.—In my view of the subject, I can, however, imagine the injury to society of a publication
which

which should traduce those illustrious names, the memory of which has warmed a nation's virtue, the *Hampdens*, the *Ruffels*, the *Sidneys* of their age; which should have for its purpose to rake up their ashes and to extinguish the still-remaining sparks, by which the flame of patriotism might be enkindled. Such a publication, I might consider as an attempt to subvert that public virtue, upon which the happiness of a state depends.

We have then examined the matter of the offence, (if I may use the expression;) let us consider its form, the mode of its communication.

The

The slander of the individual by loose words, is at most only actionable. To render them criminally cognisable, they must be connected in a sort of composition, which implies premeditation. Am I so to understand you?

L. Certainly.

L. So that to reclaim " the winged " words" from that region to which they naturally belong, and to give them a local habitation, and a name in the system of our criminal law, they must be fixed by regular prose or metre.

The definition is rather an unfortunate one, for those who have the talent of speaking

speaking in correct periods, or of making verses *stantes pede in uno.* A man might find himself uttering indictable scandal, with that sort of surprise, which Moliere's character expresses, upon discovering that he had been " talking prose" without knowing it.

L. The scandal must be *written* or *printed*; and the *publication* of it is the striking feature of the offence.

L. This feature does not, I think, discriminate it from actionable slander; for this also requires a publication.

L. By speaking;—but do you not observe the difference between these modes of publication?

L. I

L. I admit that the printing or writing of the scandal, facilitates the more extensive communication and impression of it. But you know too that the action against slander, proceeds upon the presumption of its effect on the minds, not of one or more individuals, but of all individuals, of mankind in general. If it is the degree of publicity, that is to change the nature of the injury, the fixing this offence, will be a sort of geometrical problem : " required to find the " diameter of that circle in which the " scandal propagated from actionable " commences criminal." You indeed pursue the circle till it vanishes; for I think you maintain that a *private* letter is a *publication* of the slander, it conveys to the party who is the object of it. In this instance your own principles desert you; for you will not, I hope, contend that the slander, privately communicated to the person to whom it is applied, becomes

comes more provoking from the mere circumstance of its materialisation upon paper, than when addressed to him by speaking it, however deliberately and pointedly in the presence of others. At least, you are not, I think, warranted so to contend from the experience of human nature and human passions.

L. I thank you for the expression;— it is the *materialisation* of the language, which gives a consistency and permanency to the scandal: it becomes as lasting as the material. The " winged " words" leave no trace behind.

L. Except in the minds of the auditors. This accidental circumstance may indeed aggravate the injury, but cannot alter its nature; cannot change it from a private to a public one. And, in the shape in which we at present view it, it wants the

the qualities you have now annexed to the offence; since it is evident that the permanency and further communication of the scandal depends entirely upon the party who has the letter in his power. I recur to my objection, that the mere civil trespass, the private injury, cannot become a crime by being publicly committed.

L. Not if it be an offence against the public manners?

L. This indeed would change its nature; the act would then commence an injury to the public. For, I admit that every publication, be the object of it whatever it may, that, from the expressions and ideas it conveys, is offensive to the public morals, and decency becomes from this circumstance criminally cognisable. This circumstance I admit too, might render the libel upon the character of the individual a public offence; but it would be

I acci-

accidental not essential to the injury. The misdemeanor in the case I suppose, would be punishable, not because it is an injury to the individual, which the individual may resent; but because it is an injury to the public, which the public ought to punish.

L. You admit the possibility of the offence against the public morals and virtue; and you do not exclude that of the offence against the public peace. The " tendency to the breach of it," I cannot help still insisting is the very " gift" of the offence of which we have been speaking.

L. I am endeavouring to analyse this doctrine, but when I ask you for the *reason* of it, you answer me with a technical phrase. I am examining the stamp and value of the coin, and you think you satisfy me, by telling me, you have received it for current.

L. W E

L. WE have now, I think, considered the nature of the injury, and the modes of communication which render libel a public offence.

L. I omitted to mention that it may not only be committed by *writing* and *printing* but also by *signs* and *pictures*.

L. The expression reminds me of a point, which, though within our present view of the subject, we have only touched

touched upon. It deserves however a distinct and particular examination.

It is, I think you say, immaterial to the nature of the offence, whether the *representation* be true or false.

L. Certainly; for the more true it is the more provoking.

L. To a man who has a deformed person, there is frequently nothing so provoking as the exhibition of it, by any one but himself. In such case, the demerit of the artist, would be exactly in proportion to the fidelity of his pencil. The moral painter, in course, who delineates, however truly, the ridiculous foibles, the contemptible manners, or the odious morals of another, is at least equally culpable. I speak not of the *caricature*, but of the just portrait.

L. You

L. You have drawn the neceſſary conſequence from the principle 1 maintain.

L. It would ſeem, I own, on the firſt impreſſion, that the colors of the painter, and the language of the writer, are merely the *media*, through which theſe deformities of perſon and character are viewed; that it is the object itſelf, not the repreſentation of it, which reflects the ridicule or ſcandal. The dramatic poet, the ſatyriſt, then whoſe profeſſion it is, to expoſe the vices and follies of men are criminal characters.

L. It is not the ſatyriſt, but the libeller, that incurs the penalty. The ſatyriſt exhibits the general character of the times; the libeller the particular character of the individual.

L. I understand you: you may exhibit to the age its form and pressure, but you must not hold up the mirror to the individual. You must not censure one individual, but you may censure all. The private portion of the public *odium* is infinitely small: thus divided it is felt by no one.—But satire has, for its general purpose, the correction of the public manners: may not the censure of the individual proceed from a motive equally virtuous, the reformation of its object.

L. The duty arising from particular relations in society, may render such censure justifiable. In the instance of the painter you have alluded to, it is the business of his profession to give resemblances to the persons who sit to him.

L. I accept the qualification, and shall hereafter remember it. But besides the
relative

relative duties to each other, which may arife from our particular fituations in fociety, is there not a duty to fociety in general?

L. No one has a right to conftitute himfelf the cenfor of private characters.

L. The cenfor, I fuppofe you mean, who draws from facts his own conclufions, and annexes to them criminating epithets; who forms his judgment of the individual from particular inftances, and pronounces fentence upon his general character. He who fo judges, deferves himfelf feverly to be judged. But what fhall we fay of the mere *relater?* of him who only finds facts, and leaves the conclufion from them to others. Is he equally criminal if the facts themfelves be true?

Amas d'épithetes! mauvaises louanges! says *La Bruyere*, ce sont les faits qui louent. Reverse the observation and it applies equally to censure.

L. The truth of the censure I have already said is an aggravation of the offence.

L. One might have thought the reverse to have been the case; that the offence was heightened by the falsehood of the charge, diminished by the truth of it. But I understand you—it certainly becomes more provoking to the person who is the object of it: the accusation of his own conscience doubles its severity. This rule, however, produces to the accusing party strange sort of *supererogation* of the demerit of the party accused.

L. The

L. The expression is just;—libel is an *accusation*, and ought to be judicially preferred; not in this odious course.

L. All immoralities are not judicially cognisable. There are violations of social duty, amesnable to public justice by no regular process, in the knowlege which the interests of society may be concerned. The perfidious friend—the seducer of unsuspecting virtue—the cruel spoiler of domestic happiness—the hard unfeeling oppressor of his dependants—all, all, desire the " convenient seeming" of honesty,

Da mihi fallere : da sanctum justumque videri :
Noctem peccatis, et fraudibus objice nubem.

They may well indeed resent the officious caution to mankind against them: but does the law itself prepare the disguise for such characters? does justice make common cause with the impostors in morality and religion, and in consideration for the irritability of their resentments, arm itself to avenge the detection of their profligacy?

L. Mere declamation!

L. I have, however, heard of a maxim of the civil law, which our law has I think not over looked; " *eum qui no-* " *centem infamat, non est æquum et bo-* " *num ob eam rem condemnari; delicta* " *enim nocentium nota esse oportet et ex-* " *pedit.*"

L. This reasoning has with us, its application only in the civil proceeding.

L. Hereafter I may have an opportunity of more particularly examining how far this distinction be derivable *ex æquo et bono*. When we come to view your doctrine in its further consequences, it will be be neceffary to enquire into the legality of the pofition, " that the defendant " fhall not be permitted to give that de- " fenfive matter in evidence, under the " general iffue, upon a criminal profe- " cution, which, if the fame individual " act had been the fubject of a civil ac- " tion, he might have fpecially pleaded " for his juftification." At prefent, I take this pofition to be utterly incon- fiftent with the eftablifhed rules of our judicial proceedings, rules not merely pofitive or arbitrary, but founded in the eternal principles of reafon and juftice. It is in this cafe alone, I obferve, the fuppofed criminal is deprived of thofe arms for his felf-defence, with which the humane temper of our law is in every other cafe anxious to furnifh him. The reafon for this rigorous peculiarity will alfo, I believe, hereafter explain itfelf.

L. There

L. There may be something plausible in your reasoning upon this first part of the subject: I must however suspect the fallacy of it. *Periculosum est quod non virorum bonorum comprobatur exemplis.* The position you have now been impeaching, has ever been the governing principle of that court, in which the offence is cognisable.

L. This also I may question. I will cite you a case determined in that court *.

One *Maddox*, an apothecary, had personated *Dr. Crow,* a physician, had writ-

---
* Str. 498.

ten,

ten, and taken his fee. Some perfon, who conceived, I suppose, the public to be interested in the detection of this imposture, published the fact in an advertisement. The apothecary, in confidence of your position, that the truth of the fact was no justification of the libel, had the effrontery to move the Court of King's Bench for an information against it; but did not pretend to deny the fraud with which he was charged. The case was too glaring; and the court refused the information.

L. And what is the use you make of this instance?

L. I see in this determination the triumph of the court's good sense over your un-principled position. A conjuncture could not have been devised, to put it to a severer trial, and more effectually to

force

force the confession of its absurdity. It could not have been endured, that a public impostor should proclaim his fraud in a court of justice, and obtain its interposition, for the punishment of the party whose only offence was the detection of it.

L. But you do not observe that this power is merely *discretionary*.

L. The court in the exercise of it *discernit quid sit justum per legem*; and cannot therefore be governed by your rule.

L. The prosecutor asks a favour; he must " come into court with clean " hands."

L. The prosecutor asks no favour; he denounces to the public party an offence, which

which, upon your principle, it is the public intereſt to puniſh, and offers himſelf as the mere inſtrument of the proceeding.

L. The diſcretion of the court applies itſelf to the particular circumſtances of the caſe. The rank and character of the party, in the inſtance you mention, were not, perhaps, of an importance to engage its attention.

L. " The tendency to a diſturbance " of the public peace," from whatever quarter it is apprehended, is ever of ſufficient importance to engage the attention of a court of juſtice. I collect however, from the report of the caſe I have cited, that the only reaſon for refuſing the information was, that the party had not upon oath, " denied the truth of the ſpe-" cific charge contained in the libel."

It

It is a general rule with the court, in no case, to difpenfe with this *precedent* condition. In our time, you muft recollect, that it was exprefsly required from a nobleman of the firft rank *.

L. The party however in your cafe, was not precluded from his remedy by an indictment to the grand jury.

L. If he had afterwards applied to this remedy, a fingular confequence had followed from the obfervance of your rule. The grand jury muft have found the bill upon the fame evidence which was produced to the Court of King's Bench. Upon the fame evidence, the petty jury muft have convicted the defendant. And the court might have heard this audacious impoftor infifting upon judgment, for

* Douglas 372.

the very offence, which, upon the evidence produced, it had dimiffed from its confideration; a judgment which, confiftently with its duty, the court muft have pronounced. Upon the whole, it appears to me, that this judicial proceeding reduces you to the *dilemma* of either confeffing, that your general doctrine on this fubject is inconfiftent with itfelf, or that it is incompatible with our law. For if the truth of the libel be, in any given cafe, an aggravation of the offence, in as much as by its higher degree of provocation, it has a greater tendency to a breach of the peace, it is moft manifeft that the intereft of the public in the punifhment of it, is directly in proportion to the truth of the charge; and confequently that the court, inftead of an *affidavit* in denial of the charge, fhould require one in affirmance of it. And, even, if you fhould wifh to recede from the extravancy of your doctrine, and content yourfelf with maintaining, that the truth or falsehood of the libel does not alter the nature of the offence; still, it would follow, that the court's requisition of an affidavit to a fact, which does not touch the essence of the misdemeanor, would be nugatory.

L. This would only tend to shew that the practice of the court is wrong; not that the doctrine I maintain is so.

L. I prefer the other conclusion:— That the rule of the court is right, and your doctrine wrong.

I have not, however, yet done with my case. The libel complained of was perhaps actionable; it contained a charge injurious to the party in the way of his business. Let me suppose then, that relying upon the difficulty of proving the fact charged, he had commenced his action,

action. The defendant pleads fpecially the truth of the fact for his juftification; and upon this point the parties are at iffue. The caufe goes on, the impofture is proved in evidence, and the jury find a verdict for the defendant.

The unfuccefsful plaintiff, let me now fuppofe, turns profecutor, and prefers his *indictment* for the libel. The defendant pleads the general iffue, that he is *not guilty*; and upon the trial of the *indictment* tenders in evidence the verdict and judgment in the action. Could this evidence, I afk you, be received?

L. I do not know that this point has ever been determined.

L. That enquiry is to me unneceffary; I can avail myfelf of the determination either way. If this evidence could be received,

received, the truth of your maxim is impeached;—if it could not, what will you say of its justice?

L. The notoriety of a verdict publicly given might, perhaps, make the production of it in evidence unnecessary.

L. There is a maxim in your way; *de non existentibus et not apparentibus eadem est ratio.* I will not however forget your concession, that the jury ought in their cognisance of libel, to take into their consideration facts of such manifest notoriety, that no one can be presumed ignorant of them. This, in many cases, will have the same effect as if the defendant were allowed to give them in evidence.

L. I am disposed to retract it; for it occurs to me that the private knowlege of jurors

jurors ought not to be of account in the formation of their verdict.

L. This will not exclude that which they have in common with the public.

———

The enquiry has hitherto confined itself to the spirit of the *unwritten* law; but if you consult the spirit, and even the letter of the *written* law in the only case in which it has provided a remedy for scandal, you will find that the *falsehood* of the charge is an essential ingredient to the constitution of the offence. I have endeavoured to collect the sense of our law in general, and the sense of that court in which the offence is cognisable, as to the justice of the rule we are considering:

sidering: L. now speak of the sense of the legislature upon this point. From the penning of the several statutes *de scandalis magnatum*, it is manifest, that to render it punishable the slander must be false. The offence is described to consist in "*fauxs novelles, mensonges, controveures* (inventions) *ou autres fauxes choses.*" And accordingly, the truth of the fact may be alledged in justification of the defendant.

L. The proceeding upon these statutes is *civil* not *criminal.*

L. It is both criminal and civil: it has for its object not only damages to the party for the injury sustained, but the punishment of the slanderer by imprisonment. Now the justification, it is evident, applies itself as well to the criminal

minal as to the civil object of the proceeding.

The first of these statutes * informs us of the motive for passing it. For the prevention of the discord that might arise " between the king and his people or " great men of the realm," by the " devisers of tales," the publishing of "*false* " news," is prohibited. The danger to the government from civil discord, in those times considered, the occasion was certainly of sufficient importance to engage the attention of the legislature. One is disposed however, to ask where was the necessity of its interposition. If, by the common law, the scandal that had a tendency to a mere breach of the peace, in consequence of the resentment of the individual, was punishable; surely that which threatened the very existence of

---

* Westm. 1. 3. Ed. i. c. 34.

government, was a higher degree of offence. And it is remarkable that this statute inflicts no specific penalty on the offender.

L. He is to be imprisoned till he produces "the author of the tale."

L. Agreeably to your doctrine, he would be the publisher, and consequently punishable in the first instance.

Again I observe, that if by the common law, the truth of the scandal was not a justification of it, it is singular, that in the most dangerous instance of it, the legislature should have made the offence to consist in its falsehood.

The *action* for this injury was given, not by the express words, but by the equity of the statute, as I take it, upon
this

this principle; that where an act is prohibited by law, it becomes the subject, not only of a proceeding by the public party, but also of the private party who may sustain injury from it. I except offences from which the individual receives an injury, only in common with others. I mean in general those in which he receives an injury peculiar to himself; and of these too, I must except cases in which a satisfaction to him, would be incompatible with that which the public exacts. As my instances, I mention felonies and public nusances.

With this general principle, as with others, your doctrine is inconsistent. For the libel which you assert to be a public offence, you must admit includes an injury to the individual; and this injury is peculiar to him; and his private satisfaction is not incompatible with that which the public requires. But the law you

you maintain, does not allow an action in all cases of indictable defamation of the individual. In this, as in other respects, your law is not only inconsistent with our general system, but inconsistent with itself.

In some future discussion, I may have occasion to resume the consideration of these statutes and the judicial construction of them: when my objections will probably receive from you a complete solution. The conclusion, you will observe, I draw at present is, that not only their letter and spirit, but the actual passing of them disprove the existence of your law.

There

There is one more point of view in which your reasoning ſtrikes me, which I cannot help adverting to. The general ſpirit of it may be humane, but you carry it, I think, to an extreme. You have ſo tender a conſideration for the infirmities of our nature, that you regard this injury as an irreſiſtible provocation to reſentment by violence; you do not, however, I think, allow it as a legal juſtification of a breach of the peace?

L. Certainly not.

L. But if the party defamed reſiſts the impulſe of his reſentment, you conſider his

his moderation as a juſt motive for the public puniſhment of the defamer. And thus you place the exceſs of merit in one party to the *criminal* account of the other. This perhaps is not perfect equality.— Let me however ſuppoſe, that the party defamed has himſelf been the firſt aggreſſor; that the ſcandal ariſes from the mere relation of an injury, which he has himſelf inflicted on the very party who complains of it.

L. He ought not to tell it the public.

L. His murmurs may be deep but they muſt not be loud. In your tender mercies for the feelings of humanity, you deprive miſery of its laſt reſource, complaint. But if the oppreſſed heart is denied this relief, may it not find ſome other? The ſpring compreſſed may recoil. Have you forgot your preſumptions

tions of possible resentments?—and your alarms for the public peace?—but I understand you—your maxim is just.

> Forgiveness to the injured doth belong;
> He never pardons who has done the wrong.

This poetical reasoning is not however, always to be trusted. The application of it may not be without danger, when by the use of your argument *a fortiori*, you extend the law of libels upon private persons, to libels upon public characters. The experience of human nature and of the temper of a free people might evince, that to suppress the public discussion of the acts of a government, is not always the best means of maintaining its security.

Our discussions are arrived at their proposed term. Let us recapitulate the several passages of them.

We have examined the authority of this law.

The nature of the evidence by which it is supported, and, incidentally, the legal effect of authority and precedent have been considered; considerations which have induced the necessity of resorting to the principles of the criminal department of our legal system.

With reference to these principles, the constitution of the offence of libel has been analysed.

The

The confiderations which in the view of government render it a public injury,—the truth or falfehood of the fcandal—the modes of its communication—the fe-feveral ingredients which enter into the compofition of this offence, have been examined in their feparate and combined effect.

In thefe different views this law appears not only not deriveable from, but abfolutely inconfiftent with, the principles of that fyftem of which it profeffes to form a part—and inconfiftent with itfelf.

From the refult of the whole, I conclude that the ftriking irregularities which mark this anomalous doctrine, proceed from the irregular conftitution of the offence itfelf.

This idea will more fully unfold itfelf, when in fome future difcuffion, we fhall confider the judicial cogñifance of this offence,

fence, and the confusion it has introduced between the provinces of the court and the jury, provinces in themselves perfectly distinct.

For the present I observe, in general, that you constitute the offence in such a manner, as to take the cognisance of the criminal intention of the agent, from that jurisdiction which is alone competent to it, and to transfer it to a jurisdiction which is utterly incompetent to it. When you do not suffer the consideration of truth or falshood to be of any account, in the estimation of the offence, it is manifest that you exclude the very criterion, by which human intentions must be examined. I will give you some illustration of my idea from a case *reported*, * in which the principal lines of your doctrine shall meet as in their center.

* 4 Co. 20.

THE ABBOT's CASE.

"The Abbot of St. Albans sent his "servant to a feme-covert to come to his "master, and speak with him. The ser- "vant performed his command, and "thereupon the wife came with him to "the abbot; and when the abbot and "the woman were together, the servant "(who knew his master's will) with- "drew from them, and left them two "in the chamber alone, and then the "abbot said to the woman, *that her ap- "parel was gross apparel*; to whom the "wife said, *that her apparel was accord- "ing to her ability, and according to the "ability*.

" *ability of her husband.* The abbot
" (knowing in what women repose de-
" light) said to her *that if she would be
" ruled by him, that she should have as good
" apparel as any woman in the parish*, and
" did solicit her chastity; when the wife
" would not consent to him, the abbot
" did assault her, and would have made
" her an ill-woman, against her will,
" which the wife would not suffer;
" whereupon the abbot kept her in his
" chamber against her will. The huf-
" band, having notice of this abuse to
" his wife, spake publicly of this matter.
" Thereupon the abbot (adding one sin
" to another) sued the innocent and poor
" husband for defamation in the spiritual
" court, because the husband had pub-
" lished, that the lord abbot had soli-
" cited his wife's chastity, and would
" have made her an ill woman."

The

The queſtion upon this caſe, which I have given in the words of the reporter, was, whether the defamation were of ſpiritual cogniſance.

Let me make a ſlight alteration in the caſe, let me ſuppoſe, that the offended huſband, inſtead of publicly ſpeaking the ſlander, had privately conveyed it to the abbot in a letter; had made his charge, with remonſtrances upon it, in terms of becoming reſentment.

From the *traits*, we have already of the abbot's character, it is not improbable that he might wiſh to puniſh the layman's preſumption. In his application to the ſpiritual court, it is clear he miſtook his remedy. The caſe required a *regimen* not *pro ſalute animæ*, but *pro ſalute corporis*, he prefers then, I will ſuppoſe, his indictment. The ſpecial-pleader has done

done his duty; his *innuendos* and *averments* are properly charged; he has reprefented the abbot as a character "of fingular piety, " of gravity, and exemplary manners," and has libelled *ad libitum* the defendant.

The bill is found, and the defendant anfwers to the charge of the indictment, as he well may anfwer, that he is not criminal.

The cafe of the profecutor is opened; and in fupport of it, that which the defendant is ready to admit, is proved with wonderful exactnefs, but of that which he denies no evidence is produced.

The defendant is called upon. He is in poffeffion of an evidence who had been the unobferved fpectator of the tranfaction, and he offers that defence which truth and juftice furnifh to him;—his
mouth

mouth is shut;—to what purpose indeed should he open it? his justification cannot be heard.

The *jurors*, however, may have heard something of this abbot,—they live in his neighbourhood;—his passion for *femes-covertes* may not have escaped them;—some of them may have had an experience of it in their own families.—The *jurors* have to do with nothing but the *innuendos*.

The defendant has no objection to offer the grammatical structure of the record, and the defendant is convicted.

Still there is some hope. The character of the abbot is *notorious*. (This inference from a single *faux-pas* is I own rather strained; and the general continence of the clergy of those times considered,

I

I admit the palpable anachronifm; but let it pafs.) The court then cannot be fuppofed ignorant of that which every one knows.—The court can only look at the record. It is the un-impaffioned organ by which the law pronounces that judgment which the conviction warrants.

This faithful illuftration of your doctrine, exhibits a proceeding which has for its fingular object, the exclufion of truth from a court of juftice. Can you ftill perfift in fixing fuch a folecifm, upon a fyftem which has been pronounced, the " perfection of reafon ?"

Before I conclude, I cannot help expressing it as my firm persuasion that, in the place of this exceptionable doctrine, a law more adequate to its professed object, might be deduced from the very spirit of our system.

L. Which should leave the individual unprotected, from the assassin of private reputation, and the government itself exposed, to the still more dangerous machinations of the public incendiary.

L. Which to the really injured individual should substitute compensation, instead of vindictive satisfaction: which should

should furnish to government every means necessary to its just support, without leaving to a bad administration the privilege of proscribing the virtuous citizen, who should enlighten mankind upon its designs.

L. Until your idea shall have received its comsummation, it may be of some small importance to your personal safety, not to confound the substantial distinction there is between the law *as it ought to be*, and the law *as it is*. Without this caution, like the great critic, who was himself an illustration of "the sub- "lime he drew," you may chance to furnish in your own character an example of the offence we have been discussing—The times are mild, but——

L. The age of barbarism is past;—that of cruel refinement not come, that it it may never arrive, we fhould avail ourfelves of the liberality of the prefent, for the difcuffion of truths important to the interefts of humanity.

We are confidering a doctrine which has interrupted the general harmony of our fyftem; we are examining the conftruction of that engine by which the *trial by jury*, and a *free prefs*, the very ramparts of our conftitution, have been and may hereafter be affailed:—The fpeculation may not be without its ufe.

citeth all those of the same family, kindred, or society to revenge, and so may be the cause of shedding of blood, and of great inconvenience: if it be against a magistrate, or any other public person it is a greater offence; for that it concerneth not only the breach of the peace, but also the scandal of government; for what greater scandal of government can there be, than to have corrupt and wicked magistrates, to be appointed and constituted by the king to govern his subjects under him? and greater imputation to the state it cannot be, than to suffer such corrupt men to sit in the sacred seat of justice, and to have any medling in or concerning the administration of justice.

2. Although the private man or magistrate be dead at the time of the making of the libel, yet it is punishable, for in the one case it stirreth up others of the same family, blood, or society to revenge, and to breach of the peace, and in the other the libeller doth traduce the state and government, which dieth not.

3. A libeller (who is called *famosus defamator*) shall be punished either by indictment at the common law, or by bill, if he deny it, or *ore tenus* upon his confession, in the Star-chamber, and according to the quality of the offence he may be punished by fine or imprisonment,

prisonment, and if the case be exorbitant, by pillory and loss of his ears.

4. It is not material whether the libel be true, or whether the party against whom the libel is made, be of a good or ill fame; for in a settled state of government the party grieved ought to complain for every injury done to him in ordinary course of law, and not by any means to revenge himself, either by odious course of libelling, or otherwise: he who killeth a a man with his sword in fight is a great offender, but he is a greater offender who poisoneth another, for in the one case he who is the party assaulted may defend himself, and knoweth his adversary, and may endeavour to prevent it: but poisoning may be so secret that none can defend himself against it, for which cause the offence is more grievous, because the offender cannot be easily known; And of such nature is libelling, it is secret, and robbeth a man of his good name, which ought to be more precious to him than his life, & *difficillimum est invenire authorem infamatoriæ scripturæ*, because that when the offender is known, he ought to be severely punished. Every infamous libel, either is in writing, or without writing. In writing, when an epigram, rime, or other writing is composed or published to the scandal or contumely of another, by which his fame or dignity may be prejudiced. And such libel may be published, 1. *Verbis aut*

aut cantilenis. And where it is maliciously repeated or sung in the presence of others. 2. *Traditione,* when the libel, or copy of it is delivered over to scandalize the party; a famous libel without writing may be. 1. *Picturis,* as to paint the party in any shameful and ignominious manner. 2. *Signis,* as to fix a gallows, or other ignominious signs at the parties door or elsewhere. And it was resolved *Mich.* 43 & 44 *Eliz.* in the Star-Chamber in *Halliwood's* case, That if one find a libel (and would keep himself out of danger) if it be composed against a private man, the finder either may burn it, or presently deliver it to a magistrate: but if it concern a magistrate, or other public person, the finder of it ought presently to deliver it to a magistrate, to the intent that by examination and industry, the author may be found out and punished. And libelling and calumniation is an offence against the law of God. For *Leviticus* 17. *Non facias calumniam proximo.* — Exod. xxii. ver. 28. *Principi populi tui non maledices.* Ecclesiastes 10. *In cogitatione tua ne detrahas Regi, nec in secreto cubiculi tui diviti maledices, quia volucres cœli portabunt vocem tuam, & qui habet pennas annuntiabit sententiam,* Psal. lxi. 13. *Adversus ne loquebantur qui sedebant in porta & in me psallebant, qui bibebant vinum.* Job xxx. ver. 7, 8. *Filii stultorum & ignobilium, & in terra penitus non parentes, nunc in eorum canticum sum versus, & factus sum eis in proverbium.* And it was observed, that Job who

who was the mirror of patience, as appeareth by his words, became in a manner impatient when libels were made of him; and therefore it appeareth of what force it is to provoke impatience and contention. And there are certain marks by which a libeller may be known: *Quæ tria sequuntur defamatorem famosum.* 1. *Pravitatis incrementum,* increase of lewdness: 2 *Bursæ decrementum,* wasting of his money and beggary: 3. *Conscientiæ detrimentum,* shipwreck of conscience.

www.ingramcontent.com/pod-product-compliance
Lightning Source LLC
Chambersburg PA
CBHW020131170426
43199CB00010B/722